Presto's New Pet

Damian Harvey
Illustrated by Korky Paul

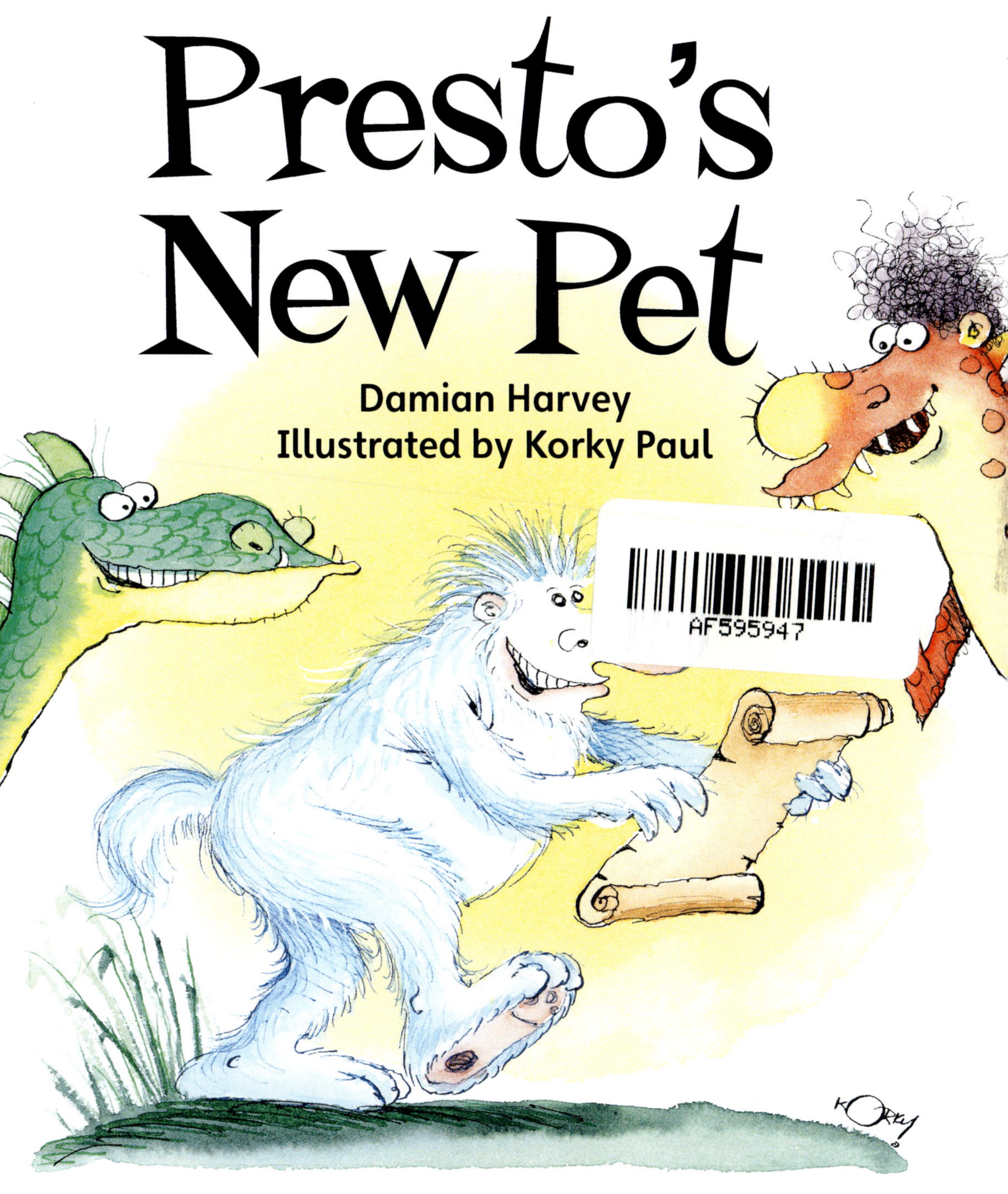

Presto the wizard lived in a tall tower at the top of a very high hill. It was the perfect place for a wizard to live, but he was very lonely.

Presto wanted a pet. He didn't want a frog or a cat. He wanted a different sort of pet.

So Presto went out into the wide world to see what he could find.

“A yeti would be a good pet for a wizard,” thought Presto.

So he went all the way to the top of the tallest mountains to look for a yeti in the snow and the ice.

But he didn’t find one.

So Presto left a note.

Later that day, a yeti read Presto's note.

"A **quiet** hill is just what I need," he thought.

So the yeti set off across the wide world to find a new home with Presto the Wizard.

Meanwhile, Presto went on looking for a pet.

"A monster would be a good pet for a wizard," he thought.

So he went all the way to the bottom of the deepest lake to look for a monster among the weeds and the fish.

But he didn't find one.

So Presto left a note.

Later that day, a monster read Presto's note.

"A quiet lake is just what I need," she thought.

"I will go and find a new home with Presto the Wizard."

Meanwhile, Presto went on looking for a pet.

"A dragon would be a good pet for a wizard," he thought.

So he went all the way under the mountains where the last of the dragons lived. He looked for a dragon in the cracks and the holes where the water drips and the rocks burn red.

But he didn't find one.

So Presto left a note.

Later that day, a dragon read Presto's note.
"A **quiet** cave is just what I need," he thought.

So the dragon flew off across the wide world to find a new home with Presto the Wizard.

Presto was tired of looking for a new pet. So he went back home to his tall tower on the hill.

When he got there he found a yeti on his hill, a monster in his lake and a dragon in his cave.

Presto had **three** new pets – and they were all **very** different!

Soon, they all became the best of friends …

and Presto wasn't lonely any more!